CALLED TO SERVE
LARRY CRAIG

Copyright © 2013 by Victory Media & Publishing

All rights reserved. No part of this book may be reproduced, stored in a retrieval system, or transmitted in any form or by any means electronic, mechanical, photocopying, recording, or otherwise without written permission from the author.

All scripture quotations are taken from the New American Standard Bible version unless otherwise noted. Copyright © 1960, 1962, 1963, 1968, 1971, 1972, 1973, 1975, 1977, 1995 by The Lockman Foundation. Used by permission.

Scripture quotations taken from the Amplified® Bible, Copyright © 1954, 1958, 1962, 1964, 1965, 1987 by The Lockman Foundation
Used by permission.

Scripture quotations marked (NLT) are taken from the Holy Bible, New Living Translation, copyright © 1996, 2004, 2007 by Tyndale House Foundation. Used by permission of Tyndale House Publishers, Inc., Carol Stream, Illinois 60188. All rights reserved.

Printed in the United States of America

Victory Media & Publishing
victorymp.com

CONTENTS

ACKNOWLEDGEMENTS	5
DEDICATION	9
WHY I WROTE THIS BOOK	11
FOREWORD	15
INTRODUCTION	17
1. Called To Serve	21
2. Know Who You're Serving, Man or God	25
3. What Is an Armor Bearer?	33
4. Developing the Spirit of an Armor Bearer	37
5. The Mindset of an Armor Bearer	45
6. The Role of an Armor Bearer	51
7. Covenant or Contract	65
8. The Heart of a Servant	71
9. The Anointing Needed to Serve	81
10. How to Handle Being Hurt While Serving Your Leaders	87
11. Who Do We Talk To?	97
12. Improve Your Serve	103

ACKNOWLEDGMENTS

First, I would like to bless and thank God, who is truly the head of my life, for giving me life and breath, and who also saw fit to save me from a life of destruction. Thank you, God, for making my life full of purpose.

I would like to thank my wife for being my rock and my strength and for never giving up on me. When I wanted to quit, you spoke into my life and encouraged me to stay the course. You prayed for me, loved me through the hard times, and walked with me. I thank you so very much.

To my children and my family, I thank you all for being with me through the transitional period of my life

Acknowledgements

when I was trying to find out who I was and for sharing me with the world. I thank you and love you all very much.

To my spiritual father and mother, Dr. R. A. Vernon and First Lady Victory Vernon, thank you for being the best spiritual parents that one could ever have. I thank you for always listening to God and for allowing me to be a part of your family, your team, and your staff. Thank you for never, ever, giving up on me, and for believing in me when I didn't believe in myself. I thank you both for never letting me quit, for helping me deal with the grief and pain of my past and helping me to believe in myself again. I love you both very much and words can't explain how grateful I am.

To the staff, I thank you all as my brothers and sisters in Christ for encouraging me to go forward with this project.

To my church family, thank you for being supportive of me, for speaking into my life, and for being there for me.

To Jennifer Wainwright and everyone who was instrumental in helping me to make this project a reality,

I thank you all.

DEDICATION

I would like to dedicate this book to my father, Clyde Dale Craig. My father was a great man and I called him *Dad*. He was forced to raise me the best way he knew how and he did a super job. He taught me, he nurtured me, and he provided for me. Through the heartaches and the pain, he never left my side and I never left his. He was there for me right or wrong. He was my best friend.

I was 30 when my father died and still acting like that little boy inside. He would call me *Son* and the last thing he told me was, "Son, you have to change now. Stand up and be a man."

Dedication

My dad never got a chance to see or experience the change of his son becoming a man, but he gave me something that I will have for the rest of my life—his voice in my heart and in my mind—*stand up and be a man.*

To my father, I know you have been on this journey with me every step of the way, and I know that you are standing up with a smile on your face and a tear rolling down your cheek, proud that your son has finally become a man. Thank you, Dad.

WHY I WROTE THIS BOOK

I shouldered the task of penning the principles and premises I believe in on the subject of servant leadership (specifically when it comes to armor bearing) with the goal of this book being a blessing to present and future armor bearers, deacons, leaders, and all who have been called to serve in any ministry. We are all servants in some form, and it is my goal to use what I have learned through my experiences to encourage you, help you understand and perfect your serve, and teach you what you need to know to become great at what you do.

In this book, you will find material that will answer many of your questions about serving. In addition, you will find information that will help you develop holistically. This book is intended to serve as a guide on your journey to become whole, as striving to become whole is integral to being an effective servant leader. You will also find practical, easy-to-apply knowledge on how to improve the quality of your service.

I have had many opportunities to travel the world with my pastor, Dr. R. A. Vernon. I've shook hands and sat at tables with some great men and women of God. In these situations, I often find myself answering questions, teaching, and helping others become better at what they do. As a result, I decided it was time to write this book.

Because of the high demand for answers to some of servant ministry's toughest questions, it is my aim to use what I have learned, what I have taken to heart, and what I have embedded in my soul, share it with those in the Body of Christ and ultimately be a blessing to God's kingdom.

I believe it's my destiny to help you reach yours. Servant leadership can be a difficult responsibility, but it can be managed, and managed well. I like to see people survive because that's exactly what I had to do.

Christianity is simply one person sharing with another person where he found the bread. Share what works for you with other people.

FOREWORD

It was Dr. Martin Luther King, Jr. who said, "Everybody can be great...because anybody can serve. You don't have to have a college degree to serve. You don't have to make your subject and verb agree to serve. You only need a heart full of grace, a soul generated by love."

If a heart of grace and a soul filled with love and service are the precursors for GREATNESS, then Larry Craig and his wife Andritta could quite possibly be the GREATEST two people I've ever met. Nearly 15 years into what I still see as a *kairos* collision, I was locked out of my first pastorate by some disgruntled leaders. I was

Foreword

lost, confused, and not sure what I would do next. Larry was basically a new convert and had come to church with his then-girlfriend Andritta. While standing there locked out on that rainy Sunday in September of 2000, he says something told him he was supposed to help my family and me and that what those leaders were doing to me was wrong. From that day till now he has never stopped helping me!

You see, that "something" that told him he was supposed to help me was God calling him to me. That's right, I said CALLING! Serving your man or woman of God is a calling that requires supernatural empowerment and anointing. In *Called to Serve*, Elder Larry Craig gives you not only the how-to of serving your leader, but the criticality of the CALL! If you sense a call to serve your pastor this is the book you have to read.

-R. A. Vernon, D.Min.

INTRODUCTION

Modern day armor bearing can be viewed through many different lenses, leaving a lot of speculation as to whether pastors really need armor bearers or if having an armor bearer is just for show. Is the purpose of an armor bearer to have someone to stroke the pastor's ego? Does the pastor just want someone in a subservient role so he or she can abuse their God-given authority, mollifying their insecurities?

We can argue over perceptions or we can just allow God to have the final say. Knowing that armor bearers are biblical should be more than enough justification for why their positions are necessary, but just in case you

Introduction

need further revelation, I'll let you take a closer look at my personal journey.

When God called me to serve in His kingdom, it was to be an armor bearer to my pastor. Since God saw fit to give me the practical gift of serving, I committed myself to this calling. (The gift of serving is covered in Romans 12:7). It is my reasonable service to the Lord according to Romans 12:1, so I chose to bloom where I was planted.

I was called, anointed, and appointed, but it wasn't until I started serving that I later became tailor-made to assist one of God's favored prophets, a visionary, who stays in touch with where God is, not where He was. Being that I was planted at the inception of our ministry, I was trained by the best—none other than my pastor himself!

I found out quickly that prayer was one of the main components I needed. You can't do a God-size assignment without God.

An armor bearer is an extension of help to the one he or she serves because he or she provides more arms. In the Old Testament, the armor bearer was more involved in the physical aspect of serving—such as fighting—than the spiritual. Today, armor bearers focus more on the spiritual.

I discovered many things during my time of service and here are a few that are key:

- **Learning My Pastor (or Leader)**

- **Knowing Their Mood and Their Habits**

- **Recognizing Their Likes and Dislikes**

NOTES

CHAPTER 1
CALLED TO SERVE

"I therefore, a prisoner for the Lord, urge you to walk in a manner worthy of the calling to which you have been called, ² with all humility and gentleness, with patience, bearing with one another in love, ³ eager to maintain the unity of the Spirit in the bond of peace. ⁴ There is one body and one Spirit—just as you were called to the one hope that belongs to your call." Ephesians 4:1-4

'Called' means to call aloud, to summon, or call forward. You have to be called to serve in the Kingdom of God. If you have been born again, you have a calling, which is simply the will of God for your life. It is the work God wants you to accomplish during the time you are here on earth. Every believer has a calling on his or her life but whether or not that calling is fulfilled depends on several factors.

First, we must recognize the call. To recognize the calling or to know the will of God for your life you must pray and seek God's face. Ask God to show you the purpose and plan for your life. This is when you open your heart to God and become willing to do whatever He asks.

Second, we must accept the call. Acceptance means to totally submit to whatever God reveals to you and go to work perfecting and honoring your call.

You must also recognize that there are two calls. The first call is a call to get prepared by purifying yourself, learning His Word, and discovering your weaknesses and your strengths. The second calling is the call to actually go and do what the Lord has told you to do. Once you accept the call, you have an obligation to work to become the best at whatever that calling is. IF GOD CALLED YOU, HE WILL DEFINITELY PREPARE YOU AND EQUIP YOU FOR YOUR JOURNEY. ALSO, IF YOU WERE CALLED YOU CAN'T LEAVE, AND IF YOU LEAVE YOU WERE NEVER CALLED.

WHAT IS YOUR CALLING?

CHAPTER 2
KNOW WHO YOU'RE SERVING, MAN OR GOD

"Obviously, I'm not trying to win the approval of people, but of God. If pleasing people were my goal, I would not be Christ's servant." Galatians 1:10 NLT

Who are you serving? Man or God? Choose this day who you will serve.

In 2004, I was a few years into my service, and I had been saved for only a short period of time. I was really trying to find my way. I was on fire, doing the work of the church, serving as one of my pastor's armor bearers and on the maintenance staff full-time. The church was growing fast and I had finally begun to deal with and try to fix some of the issues from my past.

Larry Craig

Although times were very difficult for me early in ministry, I often thought about how I was running with my pastor almost every day, doing the work of the church, and making things happen. For once in my life, I felt like I was finally a part of a bigger cause, and I was winning.

I was thrilled by all the attention I was getting. I had developed a good reputation, but paid little mind to my character. What I know now that I didn't know then is that at the end of the day, when it's all said and done, your character is what you really are; your reputation is merely what others think of you.

Finally, I stopped and questioned myself. I was in ministry, serving my pastor, but my life was not getting any better. I thought about how this was starting to affect my wife and family. It felt like my foot was nailed to the ground and at the same time like I was walking in circles. I cried out to the Lord and said, "Lord, please help me. I'm confused. My life is not changing. I'm serving in ministry faithfully and I serve my pastor. I'm trying with everything I have and this Christian walk is not working."

CALLED TO SERVE

The Lord then spoke to me and said, "You are too busy doing the work of the church and are not becoming. You don't have a relationship with Me. You don't know Me for yourself. You are breathing through the umbilical cord connected to your pastor. Cut the cord and breathe on your own because you are serving man and not Me. I kept you close to Me because of your faithfulness. Choose Me and lean and depend on Me for yourself."

I then decided to let go and let God. When I finally began to strengthen my relationship with GOD and put His principles in place, I felt like the nail was removed from my foot and I began to walk straight and move forward. I encourage you to choose this day who will you serve. It is crucial for you to know and learn the difference between serving man and serving God. Start becoming in Christ before you start doing. It's OK to start doing; just work on becoming while you're doing.

Know clearly who you are serving, because so many times we can get connected to a pastor or a leader and gain popularity, and if we are not careful, our flesh will feed off what's called *borrowed popularity*, popularity we get from our leaders. We'll become arrogant and the faster we climb up the church ladder the easier it is to leave God out and become distracted. We start to believe that man or self is to receive credit for our blessings or current position. We must stay humble and never forget that we can do nothing without God; all credit belongs to Him. Only what you do for Christ will last. KNOW WHO YOU'RE SERVING.

NOTES

Q: When looking for someone to serve in an armor bearer capacity, what attributes should I look for that will evidence that I have the right person for the job?

A: Their love for God first, the love for the pastor and first family, and their love for the ministry. Also, loyalty. Look at how committed and faithful they are to the people and things in their personal lives.

Q: As a pastor, what is the best way to train a person who is willing but has no clue how to best serve me?

A: Train them. Give them some assignments. Tell them what you need. Show them how you like things and how you like things done. Let them shadow you and encourage them to watch you closely, pointing out any particulars, habits, or idiosyncrasies you might have. Walk with them until they learn and get it for themselves.

Q: As a pastor, how do I determine what I should handle myself versus what I should allow my armor bearer to handle?

A: Delegate to them whatever you feel comfortable enough to release pertaining to your needs. Give them whatever tasks you feel will help lessen your load that you're confident they can manage.

CHAPTER 3
WHAT IS AN ARMOR BEARER?

"Do what you think is best," the armor bearer replied. "I'm with you completely, whatever you decide."
1 SAMUEL 14:7 NLT

In Chapter One, we discussed what one of the precursors to becoming an armor bearer is, and that is to be called. In this chapter, we will define what it is to be an armor bearer and discuss some of the characteristics associated with this spiritual office.

An armor bearer is one called by God to serve and help his assigned leader in ministry as well as their personal life. It is a ministry that serves pastors and other spiritual leaders in a servant/dignitary capacity. While there is some overlap in the responsibilities of an armor bearer and a traditional bodyguard/executive protector, there is one key dissimilarity. The difference between the traditional bodyguard/executive protector and the modern day armor bearer is the necessity of spiritual maturity. The modern day armor bearer acknowledges that he or she is a man or woman of God first, which is not necessarily a requisite for bodyguards. He or she understands the importance of a strong relationship with Christ, both for their personal benefit and the benefit of the person or persons whom they have been called to serve.

This is a ministry for men and women who have been called by God to support their man and woman of God spiritually, physically, and financially. Being an armor bearer is more than a profession, whether you get paid or you serve in a volunteer capacity. It is a vocation (or divine call), and as with any vocation, the expectation is that the individual serving will take their responsibility to develop and progress spiritually seriously. This means the person will have a consistent and meaningful prayer life, be committed to personal Bible study and intimate devotion with Christ, and display an attitude (reinforced by their actions) of commitment to growing further in their faith and understanding of the Word of God.

The primary obligation of an armor bearer is to release and free the time of the man and woman of God by providing practical ministry support designed to meet their spiritual, physical, and personal needs. The list of what an armor bearer does to care for their leader is quite extensive. If a formal list of contractual or covenantal responsibilities does exist, you will soon find that there is often a disclaimer (whether explicit or implied) at the end indicating "other duties as assigned." The fact of the matter is, an armor bearer should be up to the task of doing any and every reasonable thing within their means to alleviate stress, pressure, and unnecessary distractions from their leader.

Of course, what constitutes reasonable is something that you and your leader will have to come to mutually agree on, and the earlier you establish what's within reason for you, the better. As with any relationship, in order for it to be successful, you'll need to have some boundaries. You need time to cultivate your personal relationship with Christ, as well as honor any other commitments you have, such as marriage or children.

At the same time, you also need to understand that your calling comes coupled with sacrifice. Oftentimes, especially if you work for a particularly busy leader or ministry, your job will require nontraditional hours plus overtime. You can expect to be on call, and must be at the ready when your leader needs you, even if it's not during "normal" work time. Plain and simple, this comes with the territory, which is why it's important that you embrace an attitude of sacrifice for the sake of the one you have been called to.

If you have a lot of outside obligations, such as a spouse who does not support or understand the long hours you'll have to work at times, young children who need you at home, or a demanding job outside of armor bearing, you need to rethink whether God is calling you to armor bearing in this season of your life. Chances are He's calling you to something else.

CHAPTER 4
DEVELOPING THE SPIRIT OF AN ARMOR BEARER

"Then I will come down and speak with you there, and I will take of the Spirit who is upon you, and will put Him upon them; and they shall bear the burden of the people with you, so that you will not bear it all alone." Numbers 11:17

To operate in the spirit of armor bearing is an alternate way of saying you are abiding by the principles or pervading qualities of a spiritual servant. Your spirit is your attitude, what you exemplify, your character, your nature—it's who you are.

Some characteristics of an armor bearer are trustworthy, faithful, selfless, spiritually mature, morally sound, and progressive.

An armor bearer must be the gift of support. You must acknowledge that God has set you in place to provide support and assistance, whatever that means for you and your leader. There are two key words in the first sentence of this paragraph, gift and support. Among other things, a gift is something that you give to someone to provide pleasure. Using this definition, to be a gift to your leader is to lighten (not add to) their burden, alleviate stress, and otherwise afford them a sense of peace by taking care of what you can for them.

A gift can also be described as a talent, skill, or inherent ability. Relating this definition of gift to the verb support, you use what God has naturally given you to hold your leader up, to prevent them from falling. An important thing to remember is that though you may be naturally gifted in your ability to support others, you still have to work toward perfecting your gift.

There is no time to be stagnant in your commitment to personal, professional, and spiritual growth when you're serving the man or woman of God. Find ways to enhance and streamline communication between the two of you so that you're not overwhelming your leader with calls, e-mails, or texts.

To be the gift of support also means to be loyal, to have integrity, and to possess strength of character. Just as you are a gift to your leader in terms of your service to them, your leader is a gift from God—not just to you, but perhaps even hundreds or thousands of others who depend on them for their spiritual acuity, guidance, and leadership. They need someone in their corner who they can rely on completely to be ready at all times. Sometimes, they need a whole team of people, depending on the size of their ministry, but your role as armor bearer is especially significant.

Since you will be spending quite a bit of time with your leader, your loyalty, integrity, and strength of character are highly important to him or her. You need to be attentive and observe them closely, eagerly anticipating their needs and wants. They need to feel at ease around you, and know that they can count on you even when they are not at their best. They need to know that you will understand that there will be days when they may raise their voice, treat you unfairly, or expect you to accomplish a ridiculously long list of tasks.

To have the spirit of an armor bearer is to have the spirit of one who is devoted to self-improvement and development for the sake of serving one's leader in the most excellent way possible. You embrace learning, growth, progress, efficiency, and vision. You've accepted and been entrusted with a major responsibility. Be careful not to become lax or too comfortable with what God has given you.

The characteristics of an armor bearer listed at the beginning of this chapter are also paramount to your success as an armor bearer, and are fairly self-explanatory. Keep this list handy at all times. Better yet, keep it hidden in your heart, and remind yourself daily, especially during your prayer and meditation time, of what it means to embody the spirit of an armor bearer.

NOTES

Q: As a pastor, what is the best method of training I can offer a person who thinks he is called to serve me in this capacity?

A: The best training is to train them yourself. In other words, provide them with on-the-job training. Give them assignments. In addition, give them access to other resources such as books and seminars on servant leadership and armor bearing.

Q: Once on the job, is it better to add to their role a little at a time, or, submit to them a protocol of what I expect and need?

A: Give them the protocol of what your needs are and what you expect from them. Things can (and will) always be changed, added, or taken away as needed. You will be able to determine how to modify protocols as the need arises.

Q: What is the best way for a pastor to present this ministry to a group of people who may have never heard of this type of service before?

A: Show them in the Word of God so they are aware that armor bearing is biblical. Explain to your people why there is a need for a modern day armor bearer.

CHAPTER 5
THE MINDSET OF AN ARMOR BEARER

"For who has known or understood the mind (the counsels and purposes) of the Lord so as to guide and instruct Him and give Him knowledge? But we have the mind of Christ (the Messiah) and do hold the thoughts (feelings and purposes) of His heart." 1 Corinthians 2:16 AMP

It is highly important that your temperament as an armor bearer be one that harmonizes with the calling you have accepted to serve others. You must have an unassuming nature and a disposition that is pleasing to God. Be humble but self-assured, unpretentious but assertive. Above all else, it is imperative that you have the heart and spirit of your leader. In addition, an armor bearer:

- Must follow orders correctly
- Must provide strength for their leader
- Must understand their leader's thoughts and tendencies
- Must be willing to sacrifice their life and well-being for the benefit of their leader (most important)

Now, let's consider each one of the aforementioned bullet points. To begin with, you must be able to take direction and follow through effectively and without delay. As a general rule, irrespective of the circumstance or responsibility, procrastinating is always a bad idea. If this is a habit you practice, you should take immediate steps to remedy this behavior. Putting off for tomorrow what you can do today will cause you undue pressure, stress, and handicap your ability to be a skillful steward of your time. In terms of your relationship with your leader, procrastination will diminish your leader's confidence in your ability to see tasks through to completion.

Your leader needs to be able to trust that when they tell you something, it's as good as done. When you are given an instruction, it is your job to listen attentively, get any clarification you may need at that moment, and then go to work executing or carrying out the task. If the task is one with multiple parts, be sure to take notes while your leader is talking so that you don't forget anything they've said once you've left their presence. Provide task updates daily, weekly, or at some other interval you've previously discussed with your leader. Be proactive. Your leader should never have to come back to you to ask if you've completed what they've asked because they have no idea where you are on the project. I won't spend too much time here, because we'll cover this more in the next chapter.

The second bullet point suggests that you must provide strength for your leader. With the accompanying pressures of their ministry, family, and personal life, your leader will often need someone who they can depend on when they are overwhelmed or inundated by the responsibilities associated with the multiple roles they have. That's where you come in. You can provide strength for your leader in a number of ways.

Sometimes, providing strength for your leader is just being available when they need you. At other times, your intercession may be needed during a period when your leader is under spiritual attack. And still at other times, it may be your respect, loyalty, and devotion—your leader may simply need confirmation that when things get thick, they have you. Your mindset should be one that embraces the notion of building your leader up in any way you possibly can.

To be the best possible armor bearer you can be, it's important that you get to know the person you are serving as well as possible. Knowing what gets their creative juices flowing, as well as what stops them midstream, will definitely help you succeed in your position. Your awareness of what makes them thrive is just as important as your awareness of what exasperates them. What are the things or actions that your leader absolutely cannot stand? This is important to know because obviously, you would want to avoid those things and actions, and perhaps make other staff members who work closely with your leader aware as well. Do you know what kinds of behaviors your leader loves to observe? Do you regularly practice these behaviors? Being mindful of your leader's likes, dislikes, motivators, and discouragers is the only way you will continue to successfully develop your relationship with your leader.

Probably the most difficult of all of the bullet points in this chapter is the final one—the view that you must be willing to sacrifice your life and well-being for the benefit of your leader. To do this essentially means that you must place more value on your leader's welfare than your own. Does the thought of forfeiting your comfort (and in some cases safety) for the sake of someone else make you uneasy? If you are completely honest, can you see yourself putting your leader's needs before your own? These are questions you need to prayerfully consider and answer truthfully before you accept the calling to be an armor bearer.

NOTES

CHAPTER 6
THE ROLE OF AN ARMOR BEARER

"Saul groaned to his armor bearer, "Take your sword and kill me before these pagan Philistines come to run me through and taunt and torture me." But his armor bearer was afraid and would not do it. So Saul took his own sword and fell on it. ⁵ When his armor bearer realized that Saul was dead, he fell on his own sword and died beside the king." I Samuel 31:4-5

The role of an armor bearer is multifaceted, but relatively straightforward. In other words, while your position may come with a slew of responsibilities, for the most part, they are interrelated, and not all that complex. Keeping up with your leader on the other hand, if he or she is anything like the energetic visionary I serve, may not be, especially if you're not clear on exactly what is expected of you.

In this chapter, there are six attributes we'll cover as a part of the role of an armor bearer. An armor bearer:

- **Keeps their eyes on their leader and on their surroundings**
- **Carries out every plan of their leader successfully (and without question or challenge)**
- **Keeps their leader organized**
- **Serves their leader when they are angry, tired, sad, spent, and during every other fathomable human emotion**
- **Desires to see their leader get ahead in life**
- **Exalts, respects, and uplifts their leader**

We briefly mentioned in the previous chapter that an armor bearer must be observant—that they need to keep a watchful eye on their leaders. You can't serve someone effectively if you don't understand them or know them, and you won't understand them or know them unless you are attentive to their ways, attitudes, and behaviors.

Therefore, the reason for keeping your eye on your leader and their surroundings is twofold. One, your perceptiveness of their personality, attitude, and mannerisms will help you to learn who they are, and the longer you are around them, the better you'll know them. You can be a much more effective servant if you're able to forecast and address your leader's needs and wants. You can only do this, as with any relationship, if you spend some time getting to know them by watching them. You won't be an effective servant at all if you can't predict their moves at least some of the time.

The second reason why you need to keep an eye on your leader and their surroundings is because you are in your position to protect them. You have to be vigilant. Everyone will not always have your leader's best interests in mind, and you may often be the first line of defense. I am not necessarily referring to those with violent intentions (although, you'll need to be on the lookout for those individuals as well); sometimes, it may just be a person trying to monopolize your leader's time or distract them from their weekend obligations with questions, comments, or concerns that can wait or be addressed by someone else. Recognizing these individuals and preventing them from taking up too much of your leader's time and energy is an absolute must. You are a gatekeeper, especially on the all-important weekends and Bible study days when your leader needs to be focused on saving souls and delivering the Word of God. Make sure you're alert so that you can safeguard your leader from unnecessary interruptions.

The next area we're going to cover is your responsibility to carry out every plan of your leader successfully (and without question or challenge). When your leader requests that you to do something, his or her expectation is that you will get it done, and if you don't know how, you'll do the work or research required to find the way or the person to get it done. Remember, your role is to save them time, so once you're clear on the assignment, even if you are unsure as to how you're going to carry it out, don't spend a lot of time asking questions, especially if the point of your questions is to cast doubt in your leader's mind so you don't have to do what they're asking. Get as much clarification as you need, but once you're certain as to what they want, you need to go to work immediately, assuring them that you will take care of it.

Don't miss deadlines that your leader gives you. Missing deadlines breeds mistrust, and will not only compromise your integrity, but it will also cause your man or woman of God to lose confidence in your ability to make things happen.

The next area up for discussion is keeping your leader organized. I think it goes without saying that in order to keep someone else organized, you must first be organized yourself. The last thing your leader needs is for you to be all over the place when he or she already feels overwhelmed with the responsibilities that they have. If you're disorganized, you could cause your leader to feel anxiety about whether you're effectively handling his or her business, which defeats the purpose of you being in the position that you're in.

To keep your leader structured, you need to have a systematic way of receiving and transmitting information, for communicating, and for managing his or her calendar and duties. Find ways to enhance and streamline communication. There are a number of different methods for getting and staying organized; you just need to find one that works for you and your leader.

Perhaps your leader prefers to communicate by phone—always have a pen and pad handy in the event they give you instructions on the fly.

Maybe you have a leader who would rather talk in person. The same method would apply in this situation. Have your pen and pad out and be ready to write. If you have a leader who prefers to e-mail, make sure you're checking it regularly and respond as soon as you receive any message they've sent to you. In this case, I would recommend having a special folder just for your leader's e-mails so they do not get mixed in with a bunch of other nonessential messages.

Whatever approach you choose, have a plan in place for when you go back over things you've discussed with your leader throughout the day, week, or month. For example, if your leader has given you six tasks to accomplish in a given week, maybe you set a standing meeting at the week's end to discuss your progress. Also, if your leader has upcoming engagements or other obligations, this would be the time to update him or her. There is really no right or wrong way to be organized; the point is to have a system and a standard, be consistent, and if perchance your leader happens to deviate from the system from time to time, that's okay. You, however, do not ever deviate, unless you've previously discussed it with your leader,

Now, the next matter we're going to cover is a tough one. Serve your leader even when you are angry, tired, sad, and during every other fathomable human emotion. I don't have to tell you that it's much easier to say you'll do this than to actually do it. The reality is, you and your leader will not always see eye to eye. At times you'll feel overworked and unappreciated, or, because you're human, you'll have other things going on that will inevitably affect your mood, perhaps at home, or if you have another job, at work.

While your leader understands that you are not a robot, that you are a human being with thoughts, emotions, and feelings, these thoughts, emotions, and feelings are not their priority when it comes to your service and the job they need you to do.

Outside of extremes, your leader does not have time to worry about every single personal issue you have. As a matter-of-fact, because you're trained and you know what your obligation to the man or woman of God is, the majority of the time, your leader won't even know when you're having personal issues. You come to work prepared to serve with your game face on, leaving everything else at the door.

Even when your leader is the source of whatever negative emotion you happen to be feeling at any given point in time, you submit to his or her directives. Submission is profitable for us as armor bearers and servant leaders and our capacity for operating effectively irrespective of our annoyance or anger brings joy to our leaders. It demonstrates spiritual maturity and professionalism, two qualities that we must possess to be successful in our position.

The second to last topic that we'll deal with is your desire to see your leader get ahead in life. Remember, your leader in most cases will also be your spiritual mentor or guide, the one who feeds your spirit weekly. Your blessings are directly connected to them! You should earnestly desire that they do well in life, not only for your personal benefit, but certainly this is an added bonus. If your heart is pure, you'll want them to do well. If you don't sincerely hope for their success in life and ministry, then you need to do some serious self-examination to find out what your motives are, or what personal issues you have that would prevent you from wanting your leader to succeed.

Last but not least, you must exalt, respect, and uplift your leader. This imperative is impossible to carry out without the last one we discussed. You are not to worship your leader, but you are to encourage them, inspire them, and reverence them at all times. A heart plagued with jealousy, resentment, or some other emotion unbecoming of a Christian servant will prevent you from being able to do these things.

You will often be the closest person to your leader, in proximity and otherwise. It's important that you, as a part of his or her innermost circle, have their best interests in mind, and that you're always conscientious of what your presence means in their life. Your role is one that your leader will depend on heavily—you need to be sure that you are up to the challenge by being prayed up, always ready to hold the ladder steady, giving them the confidence they need to keep climbing and know that they are stable because you're there as their support (Remember, you are the gift of support).

Your leader, while he or she may joke with you from time to time, is not your friend. Know your place and your role. Your leader is your God-given spiritual responsibility. Take it seriously.

NOTES

Q: What scriptures would you use to support the basis for why this ministry exists?

A: 1 Samuel 14:6-7; Exodus 17:11-12

Q: How close should I allow an armor bearer to be to my family and me? Is this just a church position or one that would extend into my personal life?

A: This will be the closest person to you other than your wife and children. This is a biblical position that carries over to the 21st century pastor and first family. This person will become integrated into your entire personal life.

Q: How can you be visible yet remain invisible?

A: True saying—be seen and not heard. Stay in the shadow and out of the way.

CHAPTER 7
COVENANT OR CONTRACT

"A man who makes a vow to the Lord or makes a pledge under oath must never break it. He must do exactly what he said he would do." Numbers 30:2 NLT

When we first join a church we should get into ministry and begin our service. Most people don't know what their purpose is when they first get saved and join a ministry, but I believe after serving for some time, if we are praying and reading God's Word, the Holy Spirit and the Word of God will minister to us. He'll give us wisdom and discernment on what His assignment is for our lives and ministry. He'll answer questions such as: Am I supposed to stay connected to this pastor or this church? Am I here for a season or long term?

When God places you in your purpose, you will know. You will have that burning desire to do more. He wants your faithfulness. He wants to know whether He can trust you. If your calling is just for a season, that's OK because things change; however, I believe there are only a few reasons for an excusable season change in your life. Those reasons do not include when you get upset in ministry, or when things are not what you think they should be. You can't simply walk away because your feelings get hurt, or because the pastor or the ministry does something you don't like. Everything I mentioned is real and should be dealt with in decency and in order, but none of those things are enough to cause you to leave the church or your calling.

If your life changes because your job relocates, or you get married, that's different. But I believe that if you're called you can't leave, and if you do leave, you were never called.

If your destiny is connected to your leader and your church and the preaching is changing your life and making you better, then be faithful. Eventually, decisions will have to be made. Do we enter into covenant or do we sign a contract? A covenant is like a marriage. It is till death do us part. A contract expires when the terms of the agreement have been met or a certain time period has passed.

There have been times when I was so angry at my leader or the ministry and so hurt that I thought my love would never recover. Then suddenly, I return to a state of love again. No one breaks covenants because you're hurt. Covenants that are broken as a way to reduce pain destroys lives.

Some of us like contracts because they have loopholes and bailout options. It is fine to live by a contract but we must love by a covenant.

Distinguish who and what you are: covenant or contract. Some of us know right away what our assignment is. Only God can tell you that. For others, it may take some time. Make it a priority to find out right away what you are, covenant or contract.

Covenant love is a love that never lets go, never gives up, and never quits, but holds on with tenacity regardless of what the other person does or fails to do. Ask God to show you in prayer what type of connection you should have. Start asking now if you don't know.

Larry Craig

Historically speaking, a covenant, above all, was to give man a hold upon God as the covenant-keeping God. It was designed to link man to God himself in expectation and hope that God alone would be the portion and the strength of his soul.

A contract is for as long as we both shall love.

A covenant is for as long as we both shall live.

A contract calls for the signing of names.

A covenant calls for the binding of hearts.

A contract is writing your name in ink on a piece of paper.

NOTES

CHAPTER 8
THE HEART OF A SERVANT

"Now it shall be, if you diligently obey the Lord your God, being careful to do all His commandments which I command you today, the Lord your God will set you high above all the nations of the earth. 2 All these blessings will come upon you and overtake you if you obey the Lord your God." Deuteronomy 28:1-2

Jesus, the ultimate servant-leader, demonstrated what it is to have the heart of a servant during his last days on earth when He served His disciples by washing their feet. Take note of this familiar passage of scripture:

John 13:5-17
5 Then He poured water into the basin, and began to wash

the disciples' feet and to wipe them with the towel with which He was girded.

6 So He came to Simon Peter. He said to Him, "Lord, do You wash my feet?"

7 Jesus answered and said to him, "What I do you do not realize now, but you will understand hereafter."

8 Peter *said to Him, "Never shall You wash my feet!" Jesus answered him, "If I do not wash you, you have no part with Me."

9 Simon Peter said to Him, "Lord, then wash not only my feet, but also my hands and my head."

10 Jesus said to him, "He who has bathed needs only to wash his feet, but is completely clean; and you are clean, but not all of you."

11 For He knew the one who was betraying Him; for this reason He said, "Not all of you are clean."

12 So when He had washed their feet, and taken His garments and reclined at the table again, He said to them, "Do you know what I have done to you?

13 You call Me Teacher and Lord; and you are right, for so I am.

14 If I then, the Lord and the Teacher, washed your feet, you also ought to wash one another's feet.

15 For I gave you an example that you also should do as I did to you.
16 Truly, truly, I say to you, a slave is not greater than his master, nor is one who is sent greater than the one who sent him.
17 If you know these things, you are blessed if you do them.

Jesus told His disciples that He was setting an example so that they would serve others in the way He had served them.

There are a number of indicators that point to having the heart of a servant. One of them is being faithful. In this vocation, the most desirable (and valuable) armor bearers are the ones who sign up for a long-term covenant from the beginning. The ones who consider themselves to be in it for the long haul no matter what, and reassure their leaders of their plans are the ones most leaders deem indispensable.

For some of the greatest biblical examples, we need to look no further than Elisha, who served Elijah for 20 years (2 Kings 2:9).

Elijah knew the heart of the young man who had served him so well. He told Elisha that if he saw him when he left the earth, then his request would be granted (v. 10). When Elijah departed, Elisha was there to watch him being taken up into heaven in a fiery chariot (v. 11). Elijah's mantle fell from his shoulders at the feet of Elisha. It was at that time that the anointing doubled.

Joshua served Moses for over 40 years. Both men served their leaders faithfully.

To have the heart of a servant is synonymous with understanding that there will be persecution. The devil knows the tremendous impact Christians fulfilling their God-given call have on the kingdom and he also knows what an important role you play as your leader's ladder holder. Therefore, he stirs up trouble against God's servants. Everyone who lives a godly life in Christ Jesus will be persecuted, but God encourages us, *"Remember the word that I said to you, 'A slave is not greater than his master.' If they persecuted Me, they will also persecute you..." (John 15:20)*

You will often be talked about because not everyone will respect, appreciate, or be familiar with the nature of the position you hold. You may be called names like flunky, puppet, yes-man or yes-woman. You may be questioned as to why you would allow yourself to be "used" because people who don't understand will definitely look at it that way. And you should know, it is often those who are closest to you who make such comments or ask such questions, which is more hurtful than if it's someone you have no real connection with.

Realize early that this comes with the territory. The more prepared you are for persecution, the better you will be able to handle it when these situations come about. This position requires you to be impervious to some degree. To have the heart of a servant means to be equipped to handle affliction with strength, grace, and resilience.

The last indicator that we'll discuss in this chapter is being ready. Having the heart of a servant means to be in position, willing to do what is necessary, and oftentimes waiting for your next assignment. That's right; you should have an anticipatory attitude, always aiming to be a few steps ahead of your leader. You must also be capable, but having the skills to serve in this particular ministry is a close second to having the right attitude because you can be taught and trained in the areas in which your leader most needs you, but in order to be receptive to learning, you have to have an attitude of readiness.

NOTES

Q: Is there a line between being professional and being friendly (or familiar) with your pastor?

A: Yes there is. Stay in a place of respect and honor. Reverence your leader. Don't become so comfortable that you disrespect them and not fulfill your call to them.

Q: As a pastor, how do I choose the right armor bearer?

A: God will have to show you that person. It's who you and your family feel totally safe and comfortable around. Who that person is will become clear because this person will bring a sense of balance to your life.

Q: I am a servant leader, but I don't know how to separate my personal role from my professional one at my family functions. Do I serve my leader at family functions as my pastor or not?

A: A servant at heart will never be able to separate the two. Just do the best you can to balance and do not allow your professional role to interfere with your spiritual role as a spouse and parent to your husband or wife and children.

CHAPTER 9
THE ANOINTING NEEDED TO SERVE

"I am the vine, you are the branches; he who abides in Me and I in him, he bears much fruit, for apart from Me you can do nothing." John 15:5

While I would recommend that you seek God's face regarding any task you undertake in life, there are many jobs you can do effectively without His anointing. Let me assure you, armor bearing is not one of them. You may get by for a while without it, but you will inevitably fail if you are not covered by His anointing. The armor bearer ministry is a spiritual office and you cannot operate in it fruitfully with your natural ability alone. On the other hand, you can feel confident in knowing that on days when you feel naturally unsuited to handle your vocation, your anointing will carry you and empower you to do whatever it is that God has called you to do.

Can you imagine a pastor operating successfully without an anointing from Heaven? What about someone operating in the gift of healing without power? Let's bring it even closer to home: how have you managed in your personal life when you felt like you were functioning without God's anointing? God has gifted each of us with a certain amount of anointing to serve our ministry effectively.

The anointing is earned by living a holy lifestyle and seeking God continuously. It is not a one-time deal. In other words, you don't simply "get" the anointing one time and stop working for it. Your anointing is maintained and matured through ongoing communion with the Holy Spirit.

We must allow the Holy Spirit to fill us. The same Holy Spirit that empowers us to obey God will empower us to serve our leaders. An anointing from the Holy Spirit will evidence and support your service. If God has gifted you to serve, begin to recognize the anointing on your life.

I Corinthians 12:4-7 says, "Now there are varieties of gifts, but the same Spirit. And there are varieties of ministries, and the same Lord. There are varieties of effects, but the same God who works all things in all persons. But to each one is given the manifestation of the Spirit for the common good."

There are several things that the anointing will allow you to do and as you consider each of these things, you will understand even more why the anointing is so important.

One, the anointing will enable you to discern what needs to be done. Remember how we talked about an anticipatory attitude in the last chapter? Specifically, how you need to be able to think ahead and predict what your leader may need from you? The anointing plays an integral role in giving you the self-assurance you need to be able to walk in that discernment.

Two, the anointing will inspire you to go the extra mile in times when you feel like you've done enough but you know there's more to be done. There will certainly be days when you feel weak and tired and your natural ability will not be enough to carry you. In those times, you can rely on your anointing to rise to the occasion and give you the strength you need to go the distance.

Three, the anointing will embolden you to offer a word of encouragement when it's needed. You will never be able to fully support your man or woman of God spiritually if you aren't versed in the Word of God yourself. The anointing will help bring back the Word you have hid in your heart when your leader needs reassurance.

Also, because your anointing is so vital to what you do, you need to protect it. How do you protect your anointing? By living a holy lifestyle that includes regular fasting, praying, and walking in love. Doing these things will ensure that you are guarded against attacks of the enemy. You represent and are responsible for your man and woman of God at all times, thus, you have a responsibility to protect your anointing at all times.

God has placed you in your leader's life to take care of them on many different levels. Having the anointing is a fundamental necessity for being able to serve your leaders in the way that God has called you to.

NOTES

CHAPTER 10
HOW TO HANDLE BEING HURT WHILE SERVING YOUR LEADERS

"One thing I have asked from the Lord, that I shall seek: That I may dwell in the house of the Lord all the days of my life, to behold the beauty of the Lord and to meditate in His temple. ⁵ For in the day of trouble He will conceal me in His tabernacle; in the secret place of His tent He will hide me; he will lift me up on a rock. ⁶ And now my head will be lifted up above my enemies around me, and I will offer in His tent sacrifices with shouts of joy; I will sing, yes, I will sing praises to the Lord." Psalms 27:4-6

There is a strong warning throughout the Body of Christ that being hurt is oftentimes a large scar and a wound of this kind, if unattended, will penetrate deep into the soul and destroy any chance of living an abundant life in Christ.

If you've been involved in ministry for any length of time, then you've probably been hurt by someone. For some people, the situation might have been something that was easy to get over and move on to the next thing. For others, the hurts may have been deeper, leaving scars that limited your ability to trust.

Know that there will be more times than not that you will experience some kind of hurt. When you do experience hurt, go to God in prayer immediately so that the spirit of offense does not take root. Speak the Word over yourself and the situation. Go to your leader or the person that hurt you in love and gentleness and express your concerns. Keep in mind, timing is everything. Speak the truth in love; do not attack them. Allow God to give you the words to say.

Yes Christians can get hurt; Jesus was hurt. It's not wrong to be hurt, but the way you deal with your hurt makes all the difference in the world. Being hurt is a big enough problem in itself but if that hurt is not handled in the right way, bitterness will set in, and in the end it is bitterness, not being hurt that will destroy you.

It's important to deal with a hurtful situation as soon as we recognize it. If the hurt takes root, you'll approach each subsequent encounter with that same irritation and it will always be linked to some person, or some situation which will cause that root to dig just a little deeper. The deeper the root goes the more bitter it gets. Try your best to deal with whatever it is very quickly. If not dealt with, one situation can and will destroy your future happiness, joy, and wellbeing, and the collateral damage always negatively affects the ministry and the outreach of your office. Unfortunately, some people never recover from hurtful experiences because they choose not to properly deal with whatever pain they've encountered.

The hurts we face in ministry are not much different from the hurt many of us face in the workplace, marketplace, or home. Church is the one place almost everyone agrees should be safe, accepting, forgiving, and free from conflict and pain, yet in most churches, at least some elements of strife, conflict, and hatred creep in and shatter that dream for us.

It is very important to turn our focus away from the people involved and the church itself and with true focus identify the root cause of our pain. When you feel as if someone has wronged you or something has gone wrong during your service, honestly and immediately try to identify exactly what you are feeling. Pinpoint the core of your hurt—not what someone said or did to you but what it is that is really causing you pain. Then, search the scriptures to uncover what God says about what is truly hurting you. Lastly, pray and employ the scripture.

When you identify the true root of your pain, God has compassion, love, and wisdom that He'll generously apply to heal your pain. If you call on God your focus quickly becomes riveted on Him rather than on someone else. So, if your pastor, the first lady, an elder, deacon, ministry leader, or anyone else in your ministry does something to hurt you, go to them in love very quickly to address the hurt. Deal with it and begin the process of forgiveness. Don't blame God for how His children behave and don't abandon the church.

The book of wisdom from the Bible says we must guard our heart above all else for it determines the course of our life. We guard our hearts by choosing the thoughts, feelings, attitudes, and actions we hold. Guard your heart in this situation by refusing to rehearse what happened over and over and dwelling on the people who hurt you. This will take humility. God opposes the proud but gives grace to the humble. It will take a forgiving attitude and actions without any hint of vengeance. It will certainly take the power of the Holy Spirit working in and through you.

God's Word will bring healing, comfort, joy, peace, and deliverance. Remember, God will not put more on you than you can bear. He called you, equipped you, and anointed you. You are graced for this.

NOTES

Q: As an armor bearer, what do you do when you've trained apprentices but they don't seem to get it, leaving you to do everything? When I'm not there because I have to tend to my personal work and family obligations my pastor is left uncovered.

A: Armor bearing has to be in their heart. If they are not getting it, then there is a big chance the position is not right for them. This doesn't mean they are bad people, but you have to be called to this position. Until you find the right person(s), delegate some duties to a few people you trust who will be accountable to you. You may not realize it, but there is someone just waiting to be called into the game.

Q: Should an armor bearer be willing to give their life for their pastor?

A: Hard question—but yes. I believe that an armor bearer should be in a place in their heart to lie down their life for the benefit of their leader. If your mindset is not in that place then you have some serious praying to do.

Q: What is too young or too old for an armor bearer to serve?

A: I don't believe there is an age on serving God's anointed ones. Start as early as possible, as the Bible tells us to train up a child in the way he must go. You can be too old to serve as an armor bearer depending on the circumstances and needs of the leader.

CHAPTER 11
WHO DO WE TALK TO?

"Come to me, all you that are weary and are carrying heavy burdens, and I will give you rest. 29 Take my yoke upon you, and learn from me; for I am gentle and humble in heart, and you will find rest for your souls. 30 For my yoke is easy, and my burden is light." Matthew 11:28-30

Because we are imperfect people trying to become more like Christ, there will be times when we experience offense. Your leader or someone in ministry may say or do something that your spirit does not agree with, and Satan in turn uses the offense to try to lure us into sinful behavior, characterized by our reactions when we are offended.

The question was asked, who do we talk to when we're going through difficulties in ministry? When our leaders say or do something that we feel wasn't right, what do we do?

The simple answer? We are to go to God first. I believe God will always give you someone who you can confide in. It may be a spouse or another person in ministry. Everyone has someone they talk to about their personal life—their jobs, their marriage, their church, and everything in between and that's fine—we all need that person. But whom we talk to is key.

Let's talk about ministry. As an example, let's say we serve our local church faithfully and have been doing so for some time. Something happens that we don't like. Here is what we do: call our best friend (who we knew long before we joined the church) to discuss the situation with them. The problem is, this friend of ours is not a member of any church nor do they even visit a church, so they have very little to no understanding about ministry and ministry-related challenges.

Now that you've talked to them about what happened in your ministry or what your pastor said or did, they want to help you, but they don't know the right things to say. In their attempt to support you by being a sounding board and a voice of reason, they begin touting their worldly wisdom, planting bad seeds in your mind. That's one consequence. The other consequence, which is just as significant, is that you have caused them to look at church and your leadership differently because you have expressed your feelings of frustration to them, thwarting any chance of them coming to church and possibly getting saved through your ministry. The first thing they say in response to what you're going through is, "That's why I don't go to church now." You've in essence turned them off to Christ by painting a dismal picture of what it is to be saved and serving.

You must be careful who you talk to. My pastor taught us to never vent down. In other words, never talk to someone who you are ministering to or who is not in a higher place spiritually than you about your issues. Always vent up to some trustworthy person in leadership who number one, ministers to you; two, who will be honest with you and make you see yourself; and three, who will keep you encouraged.

For couples, while you may be tempted to share all your disappointments and aggravating situations with your spouse, limit what you come home and tell them because they may not be in a place spiritually or otherwise where they can handle the conversation without judgment. If you go home upset and tell your spouse who and what upset you, it will definitely upset them as well, and consequently, now both of you are upset at the church or the situation. Whereas you may have just been having a moment and needed to express your feelings to the person you love, for them it may go deeper. You will probably forgive faster than your spouse because you know your job and what comes with the territory, chalking it up to just a bad day at the office. Your spouse, on the other hand, will still be holding on to it long after your conversation.

Who you choose to disclose your ministry upsets to is critical. My pastor allows us to call him or talk to him anytime. For you, that may not be an option, or, you may simply choose not to talk to your pastor. You'll have to figure out who that person is for you. But remember; whomever it is, be mindful of what you discuss. We are trying to win souls, not lose them, and if you say the wrong thing, you may divert a person from coming to Christ.

Also, never make your ministry or your leadership look bad. It is our responsibility to keep their image guarded and others' perceptions of them protected.

To that end, never entertain anyone who approaches you talking about your pastor, first lady, or leadership negatively. Don't even engage them. Move on. It's not your job to change anyone's mind and oftentimes, those who have negative opinions don't want to change their view; they simply want an outlet to talk down about your leadership. Don't give them the satisfaction.

Don't let everybody dump their mess on you either. You are not a trashcan for other people's problems. You may choose to be a confidant for someone in ministry and that's fine, but be selective with whom you allow to come to you to talk about their issues.

GOD is who we ultimately talk to, and through our prayers and reading His Word, He will in His infinite wisdom speak to us, lead us, and give us instruction.

"I will instruct you and teach you in the way you should go; I will guide you with my eye." (Psalm 32:8)

If you are reading this book, God has called you to a place where you have not only been called, but chosen—chosen by God who knows everything about you but yet still trusts you. He knows exactly what you're going to do, what you're going to say, and what you're going to think. As you walk in this area of service in the Kingdom, you will encounter many conversations, private matters, and will see and hear things that no one else may ever see or hear. But as I said earlier, God trusts you. He trusts that you will pray!

Always remember, the closer you get, the less you must see or hear. This is a position that definitely requires loyalty and the strictest kind of confidence.

CHAPTER 12
IMPROVE YOUR SERVE

"As each one has received a special gift, employ it in serving one another as good stewards of the manifold grace of God." 1 Peter 4:10

Those of us who serve in the role of armor bearer are an integral part of our pastor's and first family's lives. We are here to make things better and to bring a sense of peace and respect in the presence of our leaders. We have to constantly think of fresh new ideas on how to better ourselves and to be more productive in our service. The only way we are able to achieve this is by constant renewal of the mind, heart, and spirit.

Always be creative. The Word of God says to pray for fresh anointing daily and renewal of the mind. We should frequently ask our leaders how we can better serve them, and as we do, try to come up with new ways on our own to improve our service. What can we do better? What can we change or add to help make our leader's life better and help him or her to be more productive?

Begin to take more off of your leader's plate. That's not being a kiss-up; that's aspiring to be the best you can be. Pray for fresh anointing daily and ask God to renew your passion. Be prompt and attentive and alert in your mind and spirit. God will not overlook your work and the love that you display in His name in serving the saints as you do. Stay obedient to your assignment and God will honor you.

If you are to succeed in your service your leader must sense the joy and victory in your life. This will assure him that he won't have to carry you physically, mentally, or spiritually.

Here are some things that will help improve your serve:

Be quick to listen and slow to speak.

CALLED TO SERVE

Be very detailed.

Be there but not there.

Be aware of surroundings.

Think of what he or she may need.

Handle only the things that you can handle.

NOTES

ABOUT THE AUTHOR

I, Larry Craig, was born and raised in Cleveland, Ohio. I met Dr. R. A. Vernon in late 1999 after being invited to his church by a female friend whom I later married. I didn't know anything about church. For that matter, I didn't even know who GOD was, but I attended the church and realized that I finally—for once in my life—wanted to change.

I continued to make progress turning my life around and attended church regularly, only to show up one morning to find the doors of the church locked. I didn't understand and was confused about what was going on at the time.

It would have been easy to walk away, but that day, right then and there, I now know that God called me to serve and help.

I looked in Pastor Vernon's eyes and asked, "Why are they doing this?"

Before he could answer, the Lord immediately spoke to me and said, "Pastor Vernon needs help," to which I responded, "I will help him and stay faithful."

I grew up all over Cleveland and later moved to the projects. I firmly believe "when you're loyal, you're loyal." I began meeting Pastor Vernon and his family whenever they arrived at church without ever asking to serve in the role of armor bearer. As a matter-of-fact, I didn't even know what an armor bearer was or what it meant at that time. I just walked in the role and it felt right, like I was doing something that I was born to do.

I remained loyal and I believe that God took my faithfulness and molded me into one of His top servants in the nation.